Love Notes from a Soldier's Diary

Craig Podmore

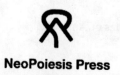

NeoPoiesis Press

NeoPoiesis Press
P.O. Box 38037
Houston, TX 77238-8037

www.neopoiesispress.com

Craig Podmore – Love Notes & Other Poems
ISBN 978-0-9832747-4-2 (paperback : alk. paper)
        1. Poetry. I. Podmore, Craig

Printed in the United States of America.

First Edition

Dedication

For a love one never inherited, for a love one will always have in the stains of one's memory, for a love one will always ache for...

Contents

Love Notes

Other Journal Entries

Love Notes

Love Notes (From a Soldier's Diary)

I

In the twilight florescence
In Florence

I give you my salutations.

Maybe granted.
Maybe ignored
Defeated expectations.

Bound by sleep,
Deep in dreamed romance,
I glance at you under stars.

Still, you do not see
Or believe in my bleeding
Heart for you.

I ache,
Thinning faith in thee.
I forsake,
Your blindness in me.

Please apply the tourniquet that you have.
Heal wounds and empty scars.

My love.

II

Once I truly believed in only darkness
Because the world had taught me it
From the day my birth cord gave way.

It's easy to ignore the beauty
Amidst gun smoke and war zones.
It's like the Hell that Dante confronted
Before his coalescence with his love,

The sufferings of all martyrs
Before they meet their gods,
The pains of puberty before
Finding the beautiful girl at the ball.

Even the progression of love
Is just as painful than having nothing at all.
The sleeplessness.
The fake fear in the stomach.
The dreams.
The wanting.

The bandages are coming off
And my soul is removed
From the intensive care unit
And off into no man's lands

Of celestial euphoria,
Hoping to seek her,
Always looking.

III

I have found you many times
In different people.
In other parts of the heart(s).
It's either in the voice,
The body, the smile
Or the soul.

It's funny how each element
Creates the one.

The one that I am in need of.

But I'm sure
I have met you before.

IV

Darling,

There won't ever be any blood
On these notes.
No trench soil stain nor
Barbwire rips.

The war and its ugliness will not blemish our light.

The only gun shot wound I maintain
Is our separation;

Being apart.

I can't wait to smell the shredded dew of
Fresh grass of home,
To see you dance in the nearby plains
With no worries at all.

Without you I fall.

V

Love,
Going
To
See
Messiahs
In the
Sky.

I will wait for you…

Lost Clippings (Fragments Found From a Soldier's Diary)

I

As bullets dance
Among the wind that bellows
I see your face.

I am in comfort.
And nothing hurts.

II

I buried a child today
And gave him a soldier's grave.

"Another one that God hasn't managed to save."

To mask the horror
We talk about our wives
And our daily lives:

The fresh baked bread,
The homely fields where we tread.
Your hands; the delicacy of silk.
The barn where we first made love,
The gramophone that plays our favourite song.

I have your photo stuck on my cap,
I am fighting for you,

My beautiful.

III

These trenches are canals
In your lungs
Leading to your heart-

I am always there.

IV

Poor guy couldn't sleep,
Oh, the weeping,
Seething with loss.
He lay, cradling an amulet
That was once his mother's.

"God love us, God love us."

V

Your voice,
I can hear it in the rivers.

Your body,
I can feel it in the leaves.

Your hands,
I caress in the trees.

Your hair,
I stroke it in the grass.

You are my mother earth.
The womb of tender life.

This is why I am not afraid.

The Heartfelt Findings of a Soldier's Yearn

I

It's cold here:
Shivering in my own shell of skin.

The cornfields
In the morning blissfully
Wake whereas I

Feel distantly afar
And a wry.

My fellow comrade
Plays his accordion
To the ghostly night fires,

As most of my desires,
Drain, refrain to gain
Once again,

That euphoria in me
Since

I last saw you.

II

My God.

Dead friends
Coat a bloody coast.

An aged man,
Screaming for his wife
And his children —

I was numb.

How can you console
A soul in a land
Of unholy?

Oh, misanthropic world.
Can we not nestle into the arms
Of those who deliver from evil?
Everything of man is death

But in you my love,
There is much beauty.

You are my house
To which I will return,

One day.

III

(To myself)

I know it's terribly frank of me
But one has these melancholy inklings
That my beloved may be in awe
Of another lover.

Who wishes to wait for a dead soldier?

A foreseeable widow,
Awaiting one another
In life or death.

IV

I was speaking to a French man
Who happened to know good English.

The village was in ruins.
Desecrated by the Nazis.

His little girl had fallen beneath
The rubble of bomb debris.

He seemed distant but I
Thought I'd offer him a cigarette.

He declined although
Amidst sorrow

He spoke to me
Unbelievably majestically

About tragedy:

Is it God's fault? No.
Is it ours? Not at all.
Is it knowledge? Maybe so.
Violence comes from the seed
Of animal instinct does it not?
Darwin declared man as animal.
If man has thought, he has the choice to control it!

(In thought)
I love you.

Why can't we control it? Huh?
The moral. The ethics.
Instead we choose to maim,
Rape and kill. Start war.
We are to blame.
But, we have choice.

Into the ether:
I love you so much

A Lonely Soldier's Scriptures

I

I've been helping the wounded.

Some of them are just soulless,
Disabled flesh of hopelessness.

The ululations of agonies,
Screaming for their Mothers,
Their wives

In pre-funereal ceremonies.

One said he could hear a violin:

She's playing 'Debussy', my wife, she plays it well.

Only for I whom could see the innards of his skull;
He has a fragment of a second to live
But what he chooses to hear in his last
Sense of living is his wife playing her violin.

All I would want is to hear you breathe right now.

II

You once said that you heard Christ weeping.

Once.

I've never heard him.
Not a whimper,

Not once,
But

I've heard the devil laugh
Beyond this landscape of
War wounds, young men dying.

Although,
For when I hear you breathe
You are the light that
Replenishes all

Demons.

III

Meditatively, transcendently
I slept in a poppy field.

The sun blinking in the bouncing
Red petals, reaching for the sky.
Glimmers of you in between –

Just as warm as the sun.

The cries of crows,
The buzzing of bees,
Capturing, trying to seize
The divine delights of nature.

It's like a painting of you.

The disposed, discordant piano
In the field my fine friends play.
The keys chant hides the gunfire nearby.
I sing within thought:

Lorna, I will be coming home to you.

IV

I nearly died today.
A bullet scathed the skin of my scalp.
It had pierced my cap, through your picture,
Complacently penetrating the centre
Of your heart.

I didn't see any God,
Only you.

You are God to me.

V

My anatomy constructed like this war zone.
Bullet strewn, desolate and degraded

But the heart of it beats
And only for you.

You can hear it,
Always.

From Lorna (The Hope, My Everything)

I

Honey,
Sorry it's taken me some time to reply.

Every night I cry,
Dishevelled and insecure,
Anxiety attacks and despair impure.

I wish it could be so simple
And say, "I love you".

There's more to it than that.
You're like a soul,
Departed, impaired and
Every night I want you.

No, I need you.

Hate this empty pillow.
This luckless isolation,
It's hard, being on your own.

II

I have met another man.
A conscientious objector,
He's hiding from the blood of war.
I can no longer wait
For a harbinger of morbidity.

I think I did love you
But not sure my soul
Deceived my emotions,
I feel out of control.

III

I had a dream the other night,
I woke up next to you.
It wasn't dawn or dusk
But the angry leaves of trees
Scratched and clanged;
Torments of the windowpane.
Although you were next to me,
You were in a wooden box –
Now, can you see?

IV

I am the Dido princess.
Do I fall from great heights?
Or do I await your return?

Please, don't be angry.
So lonely in a land
Of air raids, gas masks,
Underground tunnels
And rations.

But,
This man is no poet like you.
He's a boxer, a man of strength.
I feel secure,

Sheltered from the mourning of war.

V

(Soldier replies)

I am disillusioned my dear.
Lost, bruised, in an immense
Amount of fear.

I am scolded.
Dismembered.

The respirator,
Shutting
Down.

You were what made me breathe.

Still, you are all of me.
The ethereal brilliance,
The hope, my everything -

Each dawn is your smile:
The whole of nature's embrace.
I will never miss your immaculate,
Empyrean face.

I will be coming home to you.
You will see.

Death will not win here my lovely.

Despair (A Soldier's Prayer)

I

We loot an abandoned bar
And drank our sorrows
For the endless morrows!

We sang such obscenities:

Fuck it all, fuck the war, and fuck the Nazis,
Let's drink 'til we all fall.

I was bemused.
Disconcerted, intoxicated by many ales,
Thinking abundantly about everything –

Especially the romance that fails.

Booze depression,
Demonic, over sensitive possession.
Near sundown –

My lonely love breakdown.

The beautiful gun
Aches to touch my flesh
But this isn't the war

That has given me this menacing profundity
But my love, she's buried me lost
In this alcoholic trench of a grave.

II

The vodka numbs it.
Apply pressure to the wound.
Where it hurts.

The evil of man is now insignificant,
But the love of others I pine.

I aimlessly walk through this minefield,
Only seeing your face.

III

More drink brother.
The moonshine the farmer gave us.

I sat near two freshly dug soldier graves,
Alone on these solemn plains.

Celestially high above,
I could see far away,

Golden clouds of destruction and disarray.
They bloomed like ephemeral flowers

In a cosmos of hope.

IV

Wine. Stolen whisky. More moonshine.

Just to forget you.
Medic! Soldier down.

I think he has heartbreak sir.

V

Troops calling me sniper bait.
Mine magnet, an absolute poorly state.

Soldier, what is wrong with you? Do you want to die? Get a
Goddamn grip!

I slurred:
I'm dead anyway, she's gone. Without her, I'm frail.

Then I had a vision.
She stood before me
In the middle of this burning,
Desolate French village.
She held out her arms
Begging for my comfort.
I started to run towards
But ruined by a drunkard fall
Into a puddle of mud and blood.

Awake. She was never there.
I returned to the screaming children
Of dead mothers and the wives
Of dead husbands.

Oh, the drink let me indulge.
You don't go away.
You haunt every inch of me.
Like this evil. Here with me.

How do I overcome you my darling?

VI

I limp. Coughing up blood.
Slowly I decay.
As I drink it up, drink it up.

It's mail day.
I could just about stand.
All names alerted for those have received

From their beloved.

18

I had none.
Except for the liquid message
That resides in my bottle.
I cried alone. Shaking.
Feeling the cold even more now.

I overheard the joys of others:

She wants to get married for when I return!

The inner sinew tearing apart,
My soul fading, dissipating.

She's expecting, she thinks it'll be a boy.

The tinny gramophone with its scratchy voice
Of mediocre opera overplays its melancholy course.

My love on the red line
Beckoning the slumber
Of my pitiful existence.

I have scratched the name 'Lorna'
Onto my flask.

Life Before Horrors (Memories of a Soldier)

I

It's funny,
The past feels like a dream:

All I worried about was finding love
Because I knew I wouldn't be happy
Until one would find that love.

I met you without knowing me
But I knew I loved you already.
It was just a glimpse but that's all I needed.

It's funny how my heart jumped a little more than it usually did.

II

Before we walked to school
I left a rose on the porch of your house
Every morning

Before.

The roses I stolen from my mother's vase,
I got into so much trouble for it

But

For you it was everything.

III

I was a lonely guy,
Tucked into books, flicks and music.

You were an anaesthetic for my loneliness.
You numbed me full of love.

IV

So,
That life before horrors is
Now an irretrievable paradise –

Oh my,
I miss you so much.
Love felt so hard then
But now it's the most simplistic
Of emotions to conduct.
These horizons of hate I reside
Day in, day out,
Your face, your heart
I will always confide.

V

In the teen ballroom
One had always been alone.
Invisible, even.

The gowns had flown
For the guys who had 'it'.
I didn't have it,
Never did. Never will perhaps.

I stared at you in my own world but you didn't connect.
I asked you for a dance but you glanced,

21

Apprehensive, pensive

And denied my presence.
You were too busy with that guy
Who owned his own car and had rich parents.

It was only when you accidentally found my book
Nearby your bag that you discovered words
Of solemn romance.

My name signed at the bottom of each page
Like an amateur T.S. Elliot.

I saw you take it,
You had taken it home with you
And that night I remember because I couldn't sleep,

I envisioned you reading my words nestled in foetal position.

VI

Slowly,
We had sewn together.
You wanted to give me back my book

But

I insisted that you keep it.

It was for you anyway.

Your silky kiss on my coy cheek gave smiles
Perpetually within,

No more insecurity,
You're my new found purity.

VII

So,
Living in this horror of war
Afar from those memories
Burns deeper than a bullet wound.

The knowledge learned of losing you
Is like a lost, sepia picture of hope,
Curling in dust, withering in shadows
Awaiting a frame to be remembered forever.

The frame is to be the vessels of my impenetrable heart.
Aching, wrapping like foliage, surrounding the image
Of your angelic existence.

You kissed me for my words once.

Home is You My Love (The Soldier's Horror is Over)

I

No longer do I write to you my love
But one does pine

To an ersatz soul of mine.

I am bomb debris.
Collateral, rubble and dirt,
Discarded and hurt.

These words are now for my yearning only.
To a hung-over soul haemorrhaged
By the amour disposed
In your spirit.

This bunker, my heart,
Insecurities encased in damp concrete.

II

The hangover worsens.

Other troops and myself
Came across a projection screen in
A half demolished theatre.
Most of it was destroyed,
The auditorium severed and fragmented
Like ruined dreams.

There was one chair where
An elder woman watched this romantic film alone.

It was silent.
No music or audible screenplay.

24

Just the imagery of a couple
Staring into one's eyes.

She knew they were in love,
Her eyes glassy, lost in celluloid.
She hadn't even acknowledged our presence.

The lads and me looked at each other.
Affected by such beauty –
Amidst a war torn village,
This one lady gorges visuals
Of a true romance.

We sat down on the floor,
Disarming.
My hangover numbed
By the cinematic divinity.

I wished this for Lorna and I,
As singular droplets of melancholy
Geysered from the iris of my eyes.

Gunfire echoing not so far away
But either one of us did not flinch
As we escaped into this canvas
Of immense poeticism.

The lady uttered to me directly:

Do you wish for this too?

III

The families I have seen,
Blood stained, paralysed
By the immensity of inhumanity

That we are capable of.

The couples I have seen,
Distraught, abominated by cruelty
Unseen of a child's eye;

Holding each other tight,
The immensity of love

That we are capable of.

IV

Funerals of fire,
Blitzkrieg isolation.
Decadence, desolation,
Hopelessness and executions
For everything that inhales,

Exhales.

Prostitutes of government
Going revolver crazy.
Graves like smiles.
Little gods with death in hands.

Soviets infiltrate Berlin.
Hitler entombed,
Dressed in burial clothes.

The vodka. I feel sedated.
Abused by life.
A corpse residing in every corner.
Women. Children. All of men.

There's no Achilles here,
No Agamemnon, Virgil
Had lost his path whereas
Dante decays solemnly searching
For his love, Beatrice.

Oh, Lorna,
My paradise in thy flesh.

V

Home is on the horizon.

Nazi Germany has declared that the war is over.
After signing the settlements with the Red Army,
Many have been arrested and many have committed
suicide.

Revelations of mass murder,
War crimes one could not imagine
Discovered by the Russians.

I depart from France, Dunkirk in exactly twelve hours.

I am broken, dishevelled from all of the horror.
A wretched embodiment of failure and loneliness,
My body tremors from the alcohol abuse.

It's funny,
I don't see home when I think about it.

I only see you, my love.

Homeland (Final Entry From a Soldier's Diary)

I

There are boisterous festivities amidst the pier as we arrive home.

However, our souls are numb and empty
And the charade of smiles glimmers the pinprick
Hopes of loved ones.

Shellshock resides in our skulls,
The residue of alcohol stains our innards.
Babies play with little Union Jacks on sticks,
The ladies with home baked pies
And new, dashing frocks –

It's just all too much.
Where have all the devils gone?

My fellow comrades meet with their loved ones
Whereas I stand aside, looking for the nearest bar.
I knew you wouldn't have come, Lorna.

II

Desolation Britain.
Rubble souls and diminished civilisation.
The wheel-less pram turned on its side.
The abandoned shelters where many
Had to confide in their fears.
Children's gas masks in haunted playgrounds.
The air raid sirens still lament abundantly
For the lonely ears.

Post-blitz England,
The war is over but it still cries,

I can hear it. Always.

The half drunk bottle of bourbon in my left hand
And a picture of Lorna in the other.
I am not drowning the war out
And all of its bloodlust

But maybe the love of her.
It is too great to maintain.

The war has only just begun for me.

III

I want to meet her
But,
It's awkward.

Those Nazis were easy to kill
But to say hello to the one I love
Seems so much harder.

Being near her is like being on the frontline.
I approached the house, fragments of shells
Parade the pavements as suburban kids
Turn their hands into guns and point them towards me:

Bang, bang.

Such innocence blemished,
Ruined by perils of man.

I saw her and my stomach
Had gone off like a mortar.
Her beauty like a hidden mine,
Surprising and deadly.

We stared, in silence.

29

No words. There wasn't any.
Until a glassy molecule of sorrow demise
From the gorgeous void of her eyes.

Her open arms like a trench that would keep me from all
harm.

I sank myself into her warming torso,
She holds me tight which held me in absolute awe.

I don't know why I left you, please forgive me.

Her melancholic tone speaks fortunate truths.

You didn't my love. You never will leave me.
When the Germans were attacking,
I was fine because I was thinking of you.
When a bullet hit me, I was at ease
Because I was looking at your picture
And that healed me more than any morphine.

Touched and overwhelmed.

Where is he? The man you now love?

She had taken a step back from me.

He was caught in the blitz. He had perished. We both did.

The last three lines hurt like a public execution.
They cut my veins like the licks of a guillotine.
I have become a war victim, destroyed by lost love.

I woke, only to find myself lay on
Fragments of a fallen chapel.
The empty bottle of bourbon morbidly
Placed above my heart.

The dream had left me with a funereal emptiness.
I could not stand, shaken with the instability of drink.

What dreams apply such truths?
Truth stems from the alleys of the mind
And it is that truth I shall find.

IV

The people burn their ration books.
The hysteria of union jacks
Romanticised like a materialised
Patron saint.

They're rebuilding their lives
Whereas one is questioning his own.
Memorials on radio, live on air,
Inspirational words of Churchill
Echo throughout the ruins of its nation.

The rubble and debris like my soul;
Pieces forgotten - waiting to heal and embellish.
I have to visit her but the bar keeps me restrained.

Is she alive? In my flesh and bone she is
But reality always has its tragic smile.

V

Her house in mounds of stone and dust,
I ask a young lady nearby about the tenants
Of the house that once stood.

Are you the soldier?

Her angelical presence stunned me:

Well, yes I am my dear. Are they still alive, may I ask?

She nodded negatively,
I almost fell to my knees in despair,

31

Oh, how life is so unfair!

The Germans got them with their bombs.
I'm sorry. She left a letter for you.

For a moment, I refrained my anguish and pain
And waited for her return with the letter.

How do you know this is for me?

She knew you'd be looking.

So I did look and so I did find.

VI

Lorna's letter:

My dearest,

If you are reading this letter
Then I regret to say I have passed away.
Such sorrow of the 'morrow,
The fear of everyday events.
Civilisation falling,
Stalling, ceasing to hope
In our own humane confidence.

The blackouts:
Like my heart, bemused and lost.
I can't believe how much this war has cost -
The cost of you; priceless,
My loneliness and selfishness!
Please forgive me my darling.

On heaven's shore,
At the highest sphere,
I will wait for you.

My love is eternal,
Never ephemeral.

This poem was for you, how did I do?

If the war remains, I will live by your soul.
Block the bullets from those who you fear.
Warm you when the nights are cold.
You haven't lost me, so please do not shed
A single tear.

My dear,
I love you.
Infinitely.

VII

I slept on the spot where the house once stood.
The wind blowing the tiny spots of memories
Around me, like her breathing.
At times, even after everything had collapsed,
I could smell her presence:
Her perfumed, porcelain skin.

The absence of drink,
I needed no alcoholic comfort
For I was finally with her,

Infinitely.

VIII

May 8th 1949.

I still mourn over these words
Like prayers of other worlds.

The messiah of my love,
Her church, my heart – forever.

For once I will be simple,
Putting ostentatious words aside,
Let me confide:

I do love you.

The war however,
Along with its inhumanity
Is devoured by the power of her.

She is the V-E Day in me,
Victorious romantically
In every way.

There was one last poem I wrote for her
Whilst over at France which was returned to me
Surprisingly two years later.

Here, I end this diary with the lost poem.

IX

For you, Lorna,

Your green eyes,
The tinged, crimson halo of hair
Caressing the frame
Of you pearl-like divinity.

You're a flame,
Without disdain,
You parade your delicacy
Like a pre-Raphaelite tableau;

Awe intricacy.

You're as wonderful as any revolution.
The power of your beauty - immense!
You dominate my world -
Every second spent on thoughts of you.

Your embodiment of grace gorging me greatly.

Other Journal Entries

The Playground is Terminally Ill

This playground is terminally ill.
The scabs that are the headlines
On the breakfast table.

In the ileostomy bag
There's suffering congealed
Like dark matter

Formed in the big bang.

Ever looked unto the dying face of Fou Tchou-Li?
The abyss between the myth and the hopeful;
The coffin of God and the existence of nothing.

So we suffer to create meaninglessness.
We destroy to create a life of
Uncertainty and immense pain.

Please apply your methods of hurt
And show me the path to what
Is really

Human.

God-Awful

What is this God-awful?

Molotov post-marked ruling class,
We live in our television heads.
Give me a new October revolution
And awake the maggots

Frozen in this God-awful.

The evaporation of the workingman
Dominated by the ignorance of the middle-
Consuming the goods of despicable shit,
Buying plastic hearts in the toy shop

Is the nation's gas mask.

There are pigs in this God-awful.
Swine crucified, the notorious embraced.
The monkey was a lie like evolution
And like the credit cards we make martyrs.
This referendum is violence for the people.

Let's play the JFK
Assassination, shoot, you're it!
Let's play the Watergate,
Shush, let's go hide.
Let's play genocide,
Am I hot or cold?

Mercy, mercy, what is this God-awful?

We like bruising things that are beautiful.
We all enjoy the slow death of flowers.
The decay of man disintegrating,
Flagellating, consecrating thy legacy.

The remnants of my awakening
Like the seeds of Eden's darkest shadows,
One needs to return to the numb gallows
Of perseverance.

Nihilist Psalms

1. Denial

This Christ with rickets...

Paying my mortgage is ok.
My credit card better than Kristallnacht and
The loan is just a suicide note to get by.

I can't let you do this.
No.
I am a piggy in your farm.
No.
Give me bubonic cocaine.
No.
I am sane, I am sane.

Trivial saliva drips;
Shop windows (with on sale signs)
Exhibits gravestones.

I want to consume,
Maybe I should buy a blender.
Maybe a new car.
Maybe some cereal.
No.
I want to polish my furniture.
No.
How do my flowers look?
No.
The picture isn't central and my lawn's dying.
The soil is my blood boiled.
No.

2. Anger

Burn all churches ridden with the ideas of Bourgeois.

41

God is Bourgeois, a capitalist aesthetic.

I want to bruise you.

Maim all children of brutal consumerism.
Flesh on hooks, await the butcher for our
Bank balance.

The trains are coming.
The plan has been made.

Welcome to the house where you will find god-awful truth:

"Work makes free."

3. *Bargaining*

Ok.
I will pay you,
I'll give you everything I have.

Money piled like the corpses at Khmer Rouge,
Death is the seed of wealth.

Oh Christ,
Please, at gunpoint,
Nothing's real.

I will pay my debt, which is life.
My financial manager knows genocide well.

But,
My new designer lamp looks great.

4. *Depression*

I'm just a jester,
They laugh at my scabs.

The skulls in assembly line.
Political dilettantes with guns
Bought by the sickly rich.
20th century mass murder
On high streets, public hangings
In malls, abortions for free,
Televised slaughter on pay per view.

Violence makes the world go round.
I'm just a jester on the highest pedestal
Laughing at the world in the deathly silence
Of space.

Great entertainment that I embrace.

5. Acceptance

We are cannibals eating ourselves.
Yes, I agree.
The gallows are in our hearts.
Yes, certainly.
Dictatorships make better celebrities.
Yes, of course.
Here is a gun, please shoot.
Yes sir.
Extermination is a perfect solution.
Yes, indeed.

Now, let me sleep, let me sleep...

Pier Paulo Passolini

Collapsed sculpture of a mastermind
Resides on the barren wasteland of Ostia.
Wretched, political carcass crushed
By the evils of a capitalist fist.

Death, as in his art, brutal and relentless,
Life; the troubling sexualities of a non-conformist-

He saw society flawed, flagellated by consumerism.
His proletariat heart misunderstood like most.

The poet and a camera is well and truly mightier
Than any atom bomb.

He saw the apocalypse in people but you embraced it.
A messiah of Gramsci, a communist distilled in one's flesh.

The violent young boys, masochist loves.
The animals in them had aspects of truth

He had so wantonly desired. Jury of socialisation
Slammed the gavel on you like Hiroshima.

The crucifixion of fascists and their coprophilia,
The brutalism, the homosexuality and the man;

The sign of your own cross, a non-conformed religion.
In the slums of Rome where elements of freedom roamed

But, with criminal hegemony. His films, allegorical
statements
Against everything, celluloid fists of anger.

Salò; a cinematic, public execution for the ignorant,
His daunting Mona Lisa of cries.

The truth may have killed you my friend,
The truth all poets would kill for.

The Void of Loving

You're my canvas,
Love to paint you in my own heart
And have a part of you
That means so much to me.

You, my everlasting dear,
You scorch the endeavors of sunrays but I,
Bestow the void of loving you

Because I stare.
I stare unto.

(A memory, a dream)-

You stand alone on the shore.
A bleak day but your bright red dress
Makes a dance in the violin winds.
Amidst this grey veneer,
I pine for your attention
But realise I,
Trapped in a diving bell,
You did not know I exist.

(Another dream)-

We're holding hands in front of the world.
She's like an altar,
A church,
More spiritual,
More godly,
More immense
Than any belief known.

Then I awake,
Still loving you
In this diving bell-

The void of loving you,
Staring into me,
Becoming me.

Love Litany (Lest We Laugh)

We all hide in our abattoir masks.
Give a god a gun –
Give a man a reason to live.

Somnambulists dreaming mortars
In pantheons of nihilist praise.
Eisenhower, man of the hour,
Deflowers the innocence of knowledge.

Let's maim, kill and forget.
Lest we laugh and never regret.
Give a god a gun –
Give a terrorist a reason to smile.

The death in me is automatic.
The kill in us remains autocratic.
Mushroom cloud love
In its mass extermination.

Criminal, psychotic ovulation.

Let's maim, kill and forget.
Lest we laugh and never see sunset.
Let's maim, kill and forget,
Lest we pray and blood let.

This is a love letter.

Roads

Preacher with violence in his smile
On crossroads,

Lamenting Jabberwocky colloquial Gods
Like capitalists gorging the pence of the Jonestown
massacre.

Death is the pound
And the flesh is worthless.

Which way?

A mute revolutionary
On the hard shoulder,
Dogging the bitch
In the bush
With the crucifix,
Pissing, shitting, fucking –

Saying goodbye to the world of normalcy.

The country lane blocked by flocks of nymphs;
Sins,
Skins crawling with mites of politicians
Making orgies with the communist fist!

Which way?

Christian bastards
On dead end junctions to the edge of the earth.
Alcoholics are driving.
The poets are the wheels.
The whores are the petrol –

Guzzled by the bourgeois.

Every road I take I am in war with you.

49

I don't like you.

Full beam;
Thus, show me your true self!
Strip, carnal flesh –
Mass autoerotic deaths.

Which way?
Take me along the road to where I will purge eternally,
All over your perfectionism and catholic fascism.

Tinned Laughter

The audience claps for extermination.
Smiling. Laughing like TV show
Hosts,
Like Bolsheviks with swastika porn
And handicapped children of the state
  Like locusts on crops of solitude,
  Gorging fear with such aptitude,
Like sociopaths and vigilantes
Hiding hate in the crotches
Of social sores,
  Like assassinations of dreams
  In nuclear fellatio, Christ-tombs,
  Homemade whores,
-Ashen chimney plume.

You cough lives,
Splutter like
Bulimic butterflies
Like the third Reich
Circumcised,
Dancing in the abortion clinic.

Y Incision

Death is in the path for sure,
Although, I am lost.

Incubated in my own heart.
Ruptured innards all just because of love.

I hate love and love hates me.
This amputation of reality,
The darkness invading my veins,
Stagnating all vessels into corridors

Of nihilism and hopelessness.

My lifeless carcass may just make more sense
Than the one that lives.

So, please apply the Y Incision so that one would
Understand the notion of oneself and thus,

The existence of flesh.

The postmortem expressing
More than one did when one once
Inhaled, exhaled.

The anatomy like answered prayers
In an abattoir of stubborn meat.

Dying slowly in the face of love
Like the petal of a rotting rose resembling
The stigmata of Christ.

Slit wrists of a dawn newborn,
Exhumed from the aches of wanting,

Not needing, no more.

That Gaunt Child

Gaunt child without a God,
It has no future.

Loveless and paralysed.
And

It is blind,
A lacklustre blister
Of existence.

Lonely,
Mute cries in its discordant heavens.

It is older now but no wiser,
Just the same post-death, loveless

Mannequin of nothingness
Persevering the atom testing.

Death Row Consumerism

The condemned man requests his final meal,
He summons a menu to the guards:

Starter:

Give me the head of Jean-Paul Marat.
Fill it with oil, removing the innards.

Main:

Get me a terrorist attack served on a platter.
Dress it with ink, served cold.

Dessert

Grab some pornography and credit cards.
Burn it, well done please.

To Drink:

The froth of violence,
It will quench my regrets

Of absolutely nothing.

The guards respond:

We'll see what we can do.

In the comfort of death row,
The condemned man smiles.

Danse Macabre Eyes

In mausoleum trance
Of funereal happenings
I saw a lady dance.

In sight she
Caressed my melancholic
Innards with martyr innocence.

Her dancing feet jumped like fleas
On a hot rag like
The ones that caused a plague;

Erratic, pandemic ecstatic.
Love is a disease that
Is easy to catch.

On this sombre field
Near her grave mouth,
She posthumously paraded

With godless happiness.
Although she never woke to see me,
Even in life of kindred efflorescence!

She may have seen a shadow of despairs,
Transparent and impaired
But in death a recognition –

An affirmation
In the solemn unrequited,
That love is visible in

Danse Macabre eyes.

The golden sphere of the sun
Perforated this seraphim vision,
Framing it with such lucid grace.

The spring buds combing the humid air
As the lady nourishes the immense beauty.
She ceases to dance and then speaks:

"When your soul departs, the suffering stops
And the world is so beautiful; you see its true nature.
Now, I see you."

Her Danse Macabre eyes I value.

For Hers, Truly

Love is a viper's nest.
Heart vessel fangs filled
With venom called hope.

The fear nestles and slithers
On lonely lands, aching for
The acquainted, a second breath.

The beating organ pounds
Near snake skin, stormy clouds
Reflected on their oily surfaces.

Caressed by fork tongues
But the soul of you is heard
Amidst the hiss of such serpentines.

Still, one reaches for true gorgeousness,
Hand grappling through hellish creatures
For hers, truly

But I am bitten,
Pierced skin,
The numbness,
The pain,
The sickness –

Impending death.
For hers, truly.

Embracing the Dirge

I didn't want to pray in Bobby Sands deathbed.
The riot police in the room of thought;

Batons beating me blue in churches
Of anti-government(s) embracing the dirge.

Motorcades of dead celebrities mean more
Than revolutionaries?

I've never wanted to purge in the barrel
Of the gun that killed Guevara.

Cheap thrill pariahs and pseudo messiahs
Making coffins for the ill logic.

The painless posthumous make more money
Than the forgotten soldiers of Iraq.

Hate everything.
Love nothing.

Live like a bulletproof vest
For bullet strewn martyrs.

Mass-funereal-happiness,
Embracing the dirge.

My Heart Skipped a Heamorrhage

This harbour's cold.
There's ill logic in the air.
Demonic stabbing winds,
Callous thunder sonnets
With despots ghosts

Giving me the fear.

Oedipus eyes in my palms,
Reminiscing my ineptitude with love.
Crass crows bellow
Discordant psalms –
My heart skipped a haemorrhage.

Giving me the fear.

But this fear is a door,
A vortex of solitude and self-destruction,
A perplex portal of divine brutality.
At the end of the harbour this door stands,
Like a scab on the horizon

Giving me the fear.

So I drink
To find lonely love at the
Bottom
Of
The
Glass.

The door distorts, fades
As the alcoholic jester
Parades my blood stream.
Everything becomes nothing.

I kick that door down

And I welcome that everlasting fucking fear.

Acknowledgements

Many thanks to *Danse Macabre* for previously publishing some of the work associated with this book.

Also, I'd like to thank those who have such great words of encouragement, support and inspiration, you mean most dear to me. Without you, this work would remain non-existent, left on meaningless scraps of paper veiled in dust and age.

Thank you...

NeoPoiesis: *a new way of making*

1) in ancient Greece, poiesis referred to the process of making: creation - production - organization - formation - causation

2) a process that can be physical and spiritual, biological and intellectual, artistic and technological, material and teleological, efficient and formal

3) a means of modifying the environment and a method of organizing the self, the making of art and music and poetry, the fashioning of memory and history and philosophy, the construction of perception and expression and reality

4) an independent publisher with a steadfast goal to print and promote outstanding poets, writers and artists that reflect the creative drive and spirit of the new electronic landscape

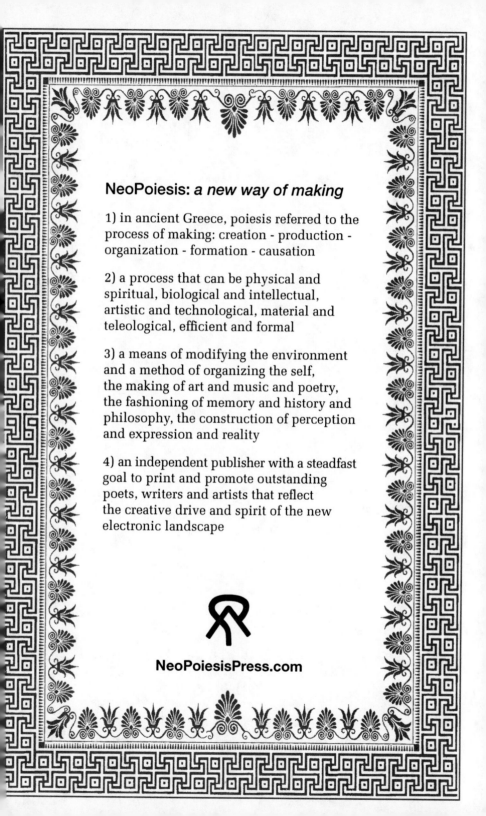

NeoPoiesisPress.com

CPSIA information can be obtained at www.ICGtesting.com
Printed in the USA
LVOW090933171111

255312LV00004B/1/P